PREPARING FOR YOUR FIRST MUAY THAI FIGHT

Everything you need to know

Jonathan James Puu

Preparing For Your First Muay Thai Fight
Copyright © 2020 by Jonathan Puu
Pu'u Muay Thai Inc.
www.muaythaiventura.com
Instagram & TikTok @PUUMUAYTHAI
contact@muaythaiventura.com
805-665-3311

ISBN (978-0-578-72016-6)

Printed in USA by 48HrBooks (www.48HrBooks.com)

Dedication

My first Muay Thai instructor, Fred Lemus, rest in peace! Thank you for everything you did and for believing in me when no one else did, not even myself. You're sorely missed.

My Muay Thai mentor, Dej "Nokweed" Sri-Ampai for giving me the knowledge to learn and to teach Muay Thai.

Table Of Contents

Introduction

This book came to be after more than a decade of experience figuring things out by trial & error. This includes my own journey as well as my competition team. I have been running my Muay Thai academy for more than 5 years which has lead my fighters throughout the world. Everywhere from dingy gyms in Mexico City, bars with boxing rings, small gyms in Los Angeles, and onto CBS Sports in the USA, TV Azteca in Mexico, Channel 8 in Thailand as well as Henan Television in China. Needless to say, I have had a ton of experience getting people prepared to step into a ring or cage for their first time up through professional level competitions.

I've been training Muay Thai since 2007 when I was 18 years old, around 13 years at the time of writing this book. I began assisting in teaching relatively fast as I began fighting after my friend signed me up for a smoker at our gym we started at. I've gone onto becoming a professional fighter as well as a ring official working with WBC Muay Thai here in North America. I founded

Preparing For Your First Muay Thai Fight – Vol. 1

Pu'u Muay Thai, a Muay Thai academy & program in 2014 and have built programs & curriculum for kids, teens & adults for all purposes: including fighting sports.

If you've never trained Muay Thai before and want to fight, I recommend you find a program nearby you to begin and use this book as a baseline to start. If you are training in a program, I recommend you consult with your Kru/Instructor/Coach along with the advice I give here as most have their own way of doing things. But this is my experience in what I've found to work and mistakes I have made with myself and my fighters that you can avoid. After all, I hope you can save more brain cells than I did figuring it out.

Chapter One
What Is Your "Why"?

There are always things that I like to bring up with people who approach me about fighting or the prospective idea of fighting. I get it, it's an exciting endeavor and the thrill is really worth it if you have the dedication, discipline & time to make it happen. Something that I always bring up for people is that when they are asking about fighting, I ask, "What is your goal with fighting?" And I'll ask you the same, what is your goal? To fight once? Become champion? Do it for fun? Be a pro fighter and make money?

There are various answers to the above scenarios but it's important to understand your "why". Also, if you're planning for just 1 fight, I highly suggest reconsidering your goal to compete a few times to get a better understanding of it. Fighting once then dumping training is a huge disservice to both yourself and your instructor. If you invest in the goal of fighting a few times, it's more likely that you'll continue training. This makes sense both from a personal development standpoint and a business standpoint for your instructor. The more experience you get, the more you can share and help build others to further YOUR understanding of what you've learned. This also keeps the program going with new experiences for new & prospective students coming in.

If you're fighting to make a living, I've got news for you, fighting doesn't pay the bills... but it is very fun, fulfilling, and challenging. That's how I ended up running a Muay Thai program and gaining a bunch of valuable experience. It's a great route to embark on but know what you are biting into before going for it.

If you're fighting to test yourself, this is a great reason! It's one that I see many people start with. They want to test themselves either mentally, physically, spiritually or a combination of all three. Either way, fighting is a great way to help develop and test those traits within yourself.

No matter the reason, now you know. I hope it doesn't discourage you but let it serve as a reality check for why you picked up this book.

Chapter Two
Time

Time is a significant factor and is something to consider. I've had many people approach me through the years about fighting. When I hand them my list of training & roadwork requirements, they usually nod and say something like, "I definitely can't dedicate time to that" or they nod and say something like, "Ok, let's do it."

Both answers can lead to fighting. The first being the "I definitely can't dedicate time to that" can be a commitment issue. If you're finding yourself here, reassess your goals and priorities in life to serve what you actually want. I could go for days here but it's better to consult your instructor on this. The latter, "ok, let's do it" is usually where you want to be before committing to the training requirements for fighting.

Time requirements to consider are:

- Training 5-6 times per week leading up to the fight
- Extra sparring & clinching leading up to the fight
- Running & roadwork 4-6 days per week depending on your program
- Meal preparation for your dietary requirements
- 1 to 5, 30-minute private lessons per week with your instructor
- Making time for unwinding and recovery from the training
- The pre, during & post-fight days
- Any required travel for extra training and the competition itself

A lot of that will fall on the responsibility of the fighter (aka, YOU) to make happen and manage along with your instructor's guidance (and this book of course).

Chapter Three
Dedication & Discipline

When taking a fight, you must be extremely dedicated to fighting. You'll miss out on birthday parties, funerals, family events, special landmark occasions, and possibly even financial opportunities outside of work. This is very important to understand as this same level of dedication is on the table from your instructor. That's right, the person who is training you, whether they talk about it or not, will be making the same sacrifices you are, and sometimes even more.

I say this from both standpoints. As a fighter, I've missed out on family occasions and been made to look stupid because of it by family (they apologized later). I've missed momentous occasions and financial opportunities because I was pursuing fighting. I've also seen this be at a detriment to a fighter's social health as well. As an instructor, I've missed out on a few family funerals and had fighters berate me because I just talked about not cornering. I didn't mention the funeral until after the fight because my goal as an instructor is to make sure the fighter is 100% focused during fight prep. Please know that your instructor may do this without you knowing. Keep this in mind when considering your dedication level.

In regards to discipline, you might be thinking, "yeah I can chip away at this for 8 weeks no problem!" Well, I've got news for you.

Preparing For Your First Muay Thai Fight – Vol. 1

If you haven't been training, you still have to learn the fundamentals of Muay Thai before even training for a fight. If you're already training, you'll have to stay ready until a fighting opportunity comes up!

Not only will you be staying prepared for fight opportunities, but you must also maintain a healthy weight for your desired weight class (more on this later). I've seen fighters lose some of the biggest opportunities in their careers because they decided to balloon up 20-30 lbs (9-13 kg for you metric folks) between fights and they were kicking themselves because of it. Now you might be thinking, "Jonathan I just want to prepare for my first fight" and I understand that, but you want to train like a professional regardless. You'll perform better and go into the competition more prepared knowing you prepared properly. I've seen some of the best fighters piss away their careers because they couldn't get their act together with their weight. Take this as your precautionary tale and feel free to thank me for it later when you get the call to be on TV.

Chapter Four
Training Gear For Fight Prep

When it comes to training for a fight, some of the most important tools you'll invest in outside of your program tuition & training partners is your training gear. I can't stress this enough, it's your body, you only get one of them. So take damn good care of it! Below is the list of essentials required for fight prep at Pu'u Muay Thai and I highly suggest you acquire all of it. They all have their very specific purpose which I'll outline later.

Training Gear Requirements For Fight Prep:
- Thai Style Steel Cup or Women's Groin Protector
- Thick shin guards designed for high-intensity sparring
- Elbow Pads
- Knee Pads
- 4-16oz Leather or Syntek Leather Gloves
- Single Mouthpiece or Specialized Mouthpiece
- Muay Thai Trunks
- Hand wraps
- Headgear (no bar across/other face shields)
- Thai Style Jump Rope
- Running Shoes
- Vagisil for the aches and pains.
- Optional: chestguard if competitions require it or if you are a youth competitor

Preparing For Your First Muay Thai Fight – Vol. 1

I'll mention again, don't get the cheap $20 pair of Century shinguards on Amazon, do get the $85+ pair of Sandee, Fairtex, Twins or Top King! Those $20 Century shinguards aren't made for high-intensity striking, your training partners won't like sparring with you as much and the chance of you getting hurt go up exponentially. The higher quality shinguards will last you much longer and will protect not only yourself but your training partners as well, it's a win-win. Save yourself the time waiting for the correct gear and get it.

For the Thai Style Steel Cup, it's an absolute requirement for my team. No if, ands or buts, you have to have it unless you're a female competitor. I don't care what the company that sold you the ultra-high-tech carbon fiber insert told you, it's not the same. Sandee, Twins, Fairtex & Top King all make great steel cups that you can use. Please keep in mind that the sizing on these is all Thai sizing, so don't get too excited when your instructor says you're an Extra Large.

Elbow & Knee pads are important to help protect both yourself and partners from hitting the hard joints. You'll most likely bang your knee or kick an elbow as will your training partners. This will mitigate injuries to both yourself and your training partners. You want to take care of your training partners as do you want to take care of yourself. Without training partners, you'll have no one to spar & clinch with.

Preparing For Your First Muay Thai Fight – Vol. 1

When it comes to gloves, I put 14-16oz as it will depend on your size and type of sparring your program does. For us, most people use 16oz gloves. I put Leather and/or Syntek as you want to make sure you have a quality glove, as chipped or ripped vinyl gloves can seriously injure your partner or yourself (think torn cornea). I recommend using lace-up gloves as they mitigate the instances of velcro burn that can open you up to infections that could potentially put you out of the competition. You want to avoid the dreaded Staph infection at all costs. I've had velcro from a glove ripped across my face several times and I'd avoid it at all costs.

Mouthpieces serve as a primary purpose of preventing your teeth from cracking together as well as keeping your jaw in a neutral position. Keeping your jaw in a position when taking blows to the head can mitigate knockouts or getting your bell rung. I've honestly used a simple $10 "boil and bite" style mouthpiece for the majority of my fight career and I started my fight career with a fake tooth right upfront of my smile. I still have said fake tooth and I've taken my fair share of damage. I've seen people visit their dentist to get molds and they turned out very poor. If you decide to go the custom mouthpiece route, find a company that specializes in making them for COMBAT SPORTS. This is key as each contact sport has different needs and combat sports are very specialized. It also goes without saying, always use the same mouthpiece and refrain from changing your mouthpiece too close to your fight if possible as they take some time to get used to breathing.

Preparing For Your First Muay Thai Fight – Vol. 1

Next on the list is Muay Thai Trunks, you'd think it would be a no brainer right? Wrong. I can't count how many times I've been at a Muay Thai event and the gym that shows up in basketball & MMA shorts are usually laughed at behind closed doors or ridiculed for not being professional. Some regulatory commissions won't even let you fight in a Muay Thai event without wearing proper Muay Thai trunks. So let this be your warning. Invest in a good pair from your academy if possible! Represent your team proudly.

Handwraps are vital to protecting your hands as there are so many small bones to jam and/or break. It's so common to jam/break these bones they actually call the break in the medical field a "boxer's fracture" due to the high instances of these. I don't care how tough you think it makes you wear some damn hand wraps. I had a younger fighter who I berated for 2 years before they finally got some. They later went on to develop some pretty damaging wrist injuries due to the previous years of not wearing them.

Headgear is important in preventing cuts and you'll most likely be having your first fight in one. So rather than complain to your instructor on why you don't like it, take it from me, get used to it. That's the game and you have to just get used to it. You probably didn't like flossing your teeth as a kid either but you do it anyway (go floss if you haven't). I recommend a headgear with basic cheek guards and no chin bar. This will serve to protect your eyes from the glove hitting it and reduce pressure & damage to your nose while sparring. Do not get a boxing style face-bar or a face shield headgear. These are very dangerous as they obscure your view when sparring.

A Thai Style Jump Rope is on this list because when I first started, most places I trained at didn't even have one or knew what they were. Chances are, your program has these available at your facility, but if they don't, you'll want to order one. These are made with a heavier tubing that will serve to build up your shoulders, chest, back, and arms for Muay Thai. I swear they aren't to punish your feet (inside joke) and they will help you tremendously. They serve a very specific purpose for Muay Thai over a generic speed rope that you see in most Western facilities.

Last on the list is a good pair of running shoes. Don't skimp on these! You will be using them a lot and believe it or not, running is an art in itself! It's also very easy to become injured from running, very often due to improper footwear and time spent on the road. I highly recommend you invest in a good pair that can set you back anywhere from $80-$150 depending on how fancy of a shoe you're looking at. Be sure to visit a running specialty store, you probably have one nearby that you've driven past at least a dozen times. If not, a simple search online should suffice to find a store. I recommend visiting the store as most running specialty stores will have you try on different shoes and assess your running stride to prescribe the correct shoe for your stride. This will help prevent training injuries down the road (pun fully intended).

Preparing For Your First Muay Thai Fight – Vol. 1

I put chest guards as optional as not a lot of places use them here in the United States for first-time fighters but there are regulatory commissions that require it or tournaments that require it. This is especially true for youth athletes and is quickly becoming the standard for kids 14 years of age and younger as Muay Thai moves closer to the Olympics. Fairtex, Twins & Sandee all make great chest guards for Muay Thai but they will set you back a pretty penny.

Chapter Five
Running & Roadwork

There are a ton of theories on running & roadwork requirements for fighters. There are trends that come and go throughout the years, there was even one that said you could get away with just doing intervals. I've tried it all and I find a combination of Long Slow Distance (LSD) & Interval running through sprint dedicated workouts and fartlek training (run slow, run fast, run hard, then repeat, etc. Google it.) to be the best for myself and athletes. I've had people laugh at me for how much I make my fighters run, but honestly, it's pretty minimal compared to the methods I've experimented with at the training camps in Thailand but is definitely "up there" in regards to mileage.

Typical running program for a high-level fighter:
- Monday: 5-mile run, LSD
- Tuesday: 3 mile run, LSD + 100 meter sprints x 8
- Wednesday: 5-mile run, LSD
- Thursday: 5-mile run, fartlek training
- Friday: 5-mile run, LSD
- Saturday: 3-mile run, LSD + 100 meter sprints x 8
- Sunday: no running

Total mileage: approximately 27 miles (~43 km for you metric folk)

Now, if you aren't already doing a lot of miles per week, DO NOT JUMP INTO THAT PROGRAM. That's an advanced program for my fighters who have built up to it. I will outline a simple formula to start running along with a base program for you to start with below. A general rule of thumb for running is to not increase your mileage by more than 5% every week. So take that for what you will, I'll outline our basic program below. You'll notice how we gradually increase time, mileage, and sprint intensity. This is how we start developing the athlete to a more advanced running routine.

Basic running program for beginners - Week #1:
- Monday: 3-mile run, LSD
- Tuesday: 1 mile run, LSD + 100 meter sprints x 4
- Wednesday: 3-mile run, LSD
- Thursday: 2-mile run, fartlek training
- Friday: 30-minute run, LSD
- Saturday: no running
- Sunday: no running

Basic running program for beginners - Week #2:
- Monday: 3.5-mile run, LSD
- Tuesday: 1 mile run, LSD + 100 meter sprints x 5
- Wednesday: 3.5-mile run, LSD
- Thursday: 2-mile run, fartlek training
- Friday: 35-minute run, LSD
- Saturday: no running
- Sunday: no running

Basic running program for beginners - Week #3:

- Monday: 4-mile run, LSD
- Tuesday: 2 mile run, LSD + 100 meter sprints x 6
- Wednesday: 4-mile run, LSD
- Thursday: 2-mile run, fartlek training
- Friday: 40-minute run, LSD
- Saturday: no running
- Sunday: no running

Basic running program for beginners - Week #4:

- Monday: 4.5-mile run, LSD
- Tuesday: 2 mile run, LSD + 100 meter sprints x 7
- Wednesday: 4-mile run, LSD
- Thursday: 3-mile run, fartlek training
- Friday: 45-minute run, LSD
- Saturday: no running
- Sunday: no running

Basic running program for beginners - Week #5:

- Monday: 5-mile run, LSD
- Tuesday: 3 mile run, LSD + 100 meter sprints x 8
- Wednesday: 4-mile run, LSD
- Thursday: 4-mile run, fartlek training
- Friday: 50-minute run, LSD
- Saturday: 1 mile run, LSD + 100 meter sprints x 6
- Sunday: no running

Preparing For Your First Muay Thai Fight – Vol. 1

Take these programs and adjust them as necessary. If you have an instructor, ask their advice on it and make sure you adjust accordingly. Please remember that many different programs have different running protocols, but if you don't have one, this is a great way to have a goal in mind for where you want to build into as you get closer to **preparing for your first Muay Thai Fight!**

Your Thai Style Jump Rope will come into play here as well. These jump ropes are integral to developing rhythm, muscular conditioning, and strengthening the feet. Ideally, you get in at least **THREE 20 minute sessions per week.** You can split that up however you want. I typically like to do it prior to training as a warm-up or after training to finish up a solid session. A small sidenote: if you can't get your roadwork in due to dangerous conditions outside, you can opt to jump rope and adapt the time to what your running would normally call for. Keep in mind, that takes practice as you have to be very consistent with jump rope in order to do interval training and sprints with it, but it can be done!

Chapter Six
Shadowboxing

If you are running before work in the morning, consider getting your shadowboxing time in after your run! It's a great way to cool-down from your run, and you're already sweating, might as well do it.

There are various types of shadowboxing and I'll describe the key use here in a moment. One of the biggest hurdles for people new to Muay Thai is getting "comfortable" shadowboxing. Hey, I get it, hitting the air and breathing "Ush!! Ush!!" in the air is a good way to make you look like a crazy person but that's part of the art. You have to understand the principles that shadowboxing plays in as you lead up to the competition.

When you shadowbox, it's the time to start developing the visualization toolset that you will use come fight day. You must learn to visualize what an attack coming at you would look like and how you would defend it. This is why it's important to have the fundamentals of Muay Thai under your belt as you have to know basic offense & defense tactics. Practice what you do know, and practice the things your instructor wants you to implement as well, this is the time to get your mind & body connected to work together to execute. You must imagine what your performing perfect technique would look like in your head and do your best to

24

mimic it physically. That is where imagination comes into play… hey, it is a martial "art" after all.

A basic shadowboxing session should last at least 10 minutes and you can break it down into rounds or do 10 minutes straight. I prefer to break it down into rounds so I have time to think about my game plan for the next round, much like you would during a fight. Sometimes, I just want to flow for 10 minutes as a cool down at the end of training and let my body & mind tell me what I need to be doing. We call this a "flow state" and takes a lot of time to develop. I'll outline a basic 3 round shadowboxing routine below. Each program I've trained in has different round lengths, I prefer 4 minutes as it lets you settle and not rush. It's also 1 minute longer than a fight round which mentally helps later on.

Basic Shadowboxing Routine:
- Round 1: Movement, evasion defense, straight punches, teeps & kicks
  - 10 push-ups between round
- Round 2: Build on Round 1, add blocking, straight knees & elbows, punches, evade & returns.
  - 10 push-ups between round
- Round 3: Building on Round 2, add in catching techniques, clinching, and higher volume combination work.
  - 10 push-ups to finish

There are various ways to shadowbox and definitely experiment! This is just the way I typically run our programs and it has a high success rate for developing the mindset necessary for fighting.

Also know that you can always shadowbox more! I highly suggest building in a lot of shadowboxing to your routine as this will help to refine movements which will save you energy, which will set you up for more success while *preparing for your first Muay Thai Fight!*

Chapter Seven
Your Training Week

Your training week will include your running & roadwork as well as your shadow boxing. In this chapter, I want to specifically address your actual Muay Thai training and what this should resemble. Ideally, for a first-time fighter, you want to be training a minimum of 2 to 2.5 hours per training day, 5 to 6 days per week. That doesn't include your running! That can include your jump rope & shadowboxing time. It depends on the program you're in.

This is what a basic training week while preparing for your first fight should look like while preparing for your first Muay Thai fight:

Monday
- Pad work or Private Lesson
- Bag work & Technique Drilling
- Sparring (15-20 minutes)
- Clinching (15-20 minutes)
- Calisthenics & Conditioning
- Stretching

Tuesday
- Pad work or Private Lesson
- Bag work & Technique Drilling
- Clinching (30 minutes)
- Calisthenics & Conditioning

- Stretching

Wednesday
- Pad work or Private Lesson
- Bag work & Technique Drilling
- Sparring (30-45 minutes)
- Clinching (10-15 minutes)
- Calisthenics & Conditioning
- Stretching

Thursday
- Pad work or Private Lesson
- Bag work & Technique Drilling
- Clinching (30 minutes)
- Calisthenics & Conditioning
- Stretching

Friday/Saturday
You can do this all on Friday or Saturday or split it up through both days.
- Padwork OR Bag work & Technique Drilling
- Sparring (30-45 minutes)
- Clinching (30 minutes)
- Calisthenics & Conditioning
- Stretching

Sunday
Rest & recovery/active recovery/stretching

Notice how we do a higher volume of Sparring & Clinching variations throughout the week. This allows us to push our bodies and minimize injuries from sparring. As you get to 3 weeks away from your fight, you start increasing the intensity of your training sessions. There are various ways to do this, the most common for my team is through hard clinch training & conditioning drills. I'll break those down in another chapter.

This is what a typical fight week at our program will look like, we will assume that your first Muay Thai fight is on Saturday and that weigh-in is the same day. You'll keep your roadwork the same until Wednesday, the only change you have is that you WILL NOT BE DOING SPRINTS. It's ideal that the week of your flight, you don't hold pads too much for various reasons which we can discuss later.

Week of your First Muay Thai fight:

Monday
- Pad work or Private Lesson
- Bag work & Technique Drilling
- VERY LIGHT Clinching (15 minutes)
- Calisthenics & Conditioning
- Shadowboxing to cooldown
- Stretching

Tuesday
- Pad work or Private Lesson
- Bag work & Technique Drilling

- VERY LIGHT offense & defense drills (15 minutes)
- Calisthenics & Conditioning
- Shadowboxing to cooldown
- Stretching

Wednesday

- Padwork or Private Lesson
- Bag work
- Calisthenics & Conditioning
- Shadowboxing to cooldown
- Stretching

Thursday

- Rest & Recovery
- Still go to the academy to hang out with the team

Friday

- Rest & Recovery
- Still go to the academy to hang out with the team

Saturday

- Your First Muay Thai Fight!

In the above week, everything has a very specific mental & physical purpose. No wasted energy should be expended the week of the fight. The next topic there is a hot debate on, but it's something I'd like to address how we run things and how I was taught by my Thai trainers.

Preparing For Your First Muay Thai Fight – Vol. 1

For the 2 weeks leading up to a fight, no sex or masturbation is allowed. Yes, you read that right. There are no ifs, ands or buts about it. I was skeptical of this at first, but I'd literally see my Thai trainers pick people apart and figure out who was having sex leading up to a fight. I would usually be aware as it was my friends who I knew were doing the deed when they shouldn't have been. No one told our trainer, he just knew. So whether you think it's bullshit or not, that's the rule we have for our team.

Chapter Eight
Pad Work & Private Lessons

Since you're reading this book, I'll assume that you're training in a Western-style program that is not in Thailand. If you are in Thailand and reading this, just do what your trainer tells you! In Western-style programs, you'll often have other students who hold for each other, which is awesome! Pad Holding is an art in and of itself which some students will hone in on overtime. Most likely though, your instructors are the people you want to get the time in with leading up to your first Muay Thai fight.

This is what your Thai Pad rounds should mimic throughout the week:

Monday/Tuesday/Wednesday/Thursday/Friday/Saturday
4 or 5 rounds, at 3 to 5 minutes per round, 1-minute rest between
- 3 to 5 rounds of Thai Pads
- 0 to 2 Focus Mitt rounds
- 10 Body Kicks each leg at the end of every round
- 10 Body Kicks each leg at the between of rounds 2 through 5
- 20 V-Sits between each round

It's a very basic formula but one that is important. Basics win fights and it's generally the same formula with slight variations at every program I've ever been to. It's very important that your pad

32

holder mimics throwing strikes to check your defense and knows how to hold properly for return shots. The purpose of pad holding is to develop the fighter to always be on offense & defense. If you defend something, you should be able to return right away. Make sure you can grab to clinch or have your pad holder try to engage in the clinch while they are holding for you.

The most common mistake I'll see from students holding for each other, is that the pad holder will just sit there and hit the fighter without holding for return strikes. This will just teach you to be a really good punching bag (NOT GOOD), this is why I suggest you seek private lessons from your instructor. In our program, it's required 4-6 weeks out from fight day that fighters get AT LEAST 1 private lesson per week from designated instructors. This is usually the instructors who will be present at your fight or who have the most experience developing a fighter both technically & mentally.

Chapter Nine
Bag Work & Conditioning Drills

Really bag work can be a completely separate book on its own, so I will do my best to condense the basic idea of bag work and some drills you can do per the training criteria. The main use of bag work is to develop timing, technique, power & conditioning of the body. You'll find the top Muay Thai fighters pretty much "play" with a heavy bag for extended periods of time. This is a great way to think of it rather than in rounds. This of course is assuming you're not doing the bag work for conditioning purposes.

Basic Bag Work "Play" - you can chunk into rounds or just time

- 2 Minutes working on Lead Leg Kicks (teeps, body, leg kicks, etc)
- 2 Minutes working on Rear Leg Kicks (teeps, body, leg kicks, etc)
- 2 Minutes working on Punch & Kick Only
- 2 Minutes working close to bag with Punches, Knees & Elbows
- 2 Minutes working on Defense & Returns
- 5 Minutes working on all Muay Thai weapons, offense & defense, timing, freestyle, etc.
- Repeat 5-minute rounds as necessary

Preparing For Your First Muay Thai Fight – Vol. 1

Bag Drills To Do Every Day

Teep Drill
- Alternating Teeps for 50 (25 each leg)
- Hanging Leg Teep, 25 with left leg, 25 with right
- Alternating Teeps for 50 (25 each leg)

Teep To Body Kick
- Lead Teep to Rear Body Kick 10 times
- Rear Teep to Lead Body Kick 10 times
- Lead Teep to Lead Body Switch Kick 10 times
- Rear Teep to Rear body Kick 10 times

Low-Med-High Kick
- Leg Kick to Body Kick to High Kick, rapid succession with good technique & balance. Do for 10 times each leg.

Skip Knees - Conditioning
- 2 sets of 50, add additional set every day or two until you are doing 300+ skip knees every day
- 20 push-ups between sets (optional)

Check & Return Kicks - Conditioning
- Rear Check & Rear Body Kick 50 times
- Lead Check & Switch Kick 50 Times

Single-Double Kicks - Conditioning
- Single Power Kick, Double Speed Kick
- Do 50 with each leg

Single Kicks For Power - Conditioning
- 50 Each Leg, good balance every time

Speed Kicks - Conditioning
- 50 Each Leg

Non-Stop Punching - Conditioning
- Jab-Cross while stepping in place for 3 minutes, consistent pace

Now, if you aren't doing all of the bag drills above, start by adding 1-2 per session to build into the program. If you start right away, you probably won't be able to do it the next day, which defeats the purpose of training. Build steadily like a fighter building momentum in a fight!

Tabata Bag rounds (HIIT) - Conditioning
- Set a timer for 20 seconds of work, 10 seconds of rest for a total of 4 MINUTES
- The goal is to work at max capacity for the full 20 seconds and do your best to get your heart rate down and oxygenate your blood (breathing) during the 10-second break.
- Repeat for 1-4 rounds

Our team will do these 2-3 times per week depending on the training cycle at the athlete's recovery.

Chapter Ten
Calisthenics

There are many calisthenic exercises you must use to prepare for your first Muay Thai fight. I'll outline the ones we use below as well as some stuff we introduce 3 weeks out to build more conditioning for the body.

Every Day Calisthenics

- Push-ups, sets of 20, 10 or 5, repeat until you get to 200
- Sit-ups/crunches, sets of 25, repeat until you get to 300
- Pull-ups, sets of 10 or 5, repeat until you get to 50, the goal is 100

Foundation:

I highly recommend you implement these if you aren't, do every session.

- Squats, sets of 20, repeat until you get to 100
- Lunges, sets of 20, repeat until you get 100 each leg
- Calf Raises, 50 repetitions

In the above calisthenic routine, it's important to listen to your body! Again, ease into the routine slowly. If you're not doing any push-ups, shoot for getting to 50 push-ups your first day! Slowly increase, just like with your running.

Abdominal Conditioning, 3 weeks out, stop using 5 days before the fight.

- 25 Sit-Ups while a partner smacks your midsection with a Thai pad between every repetition.
  - It's important that your partner hits all over your midsection as you want to make sure you are conditioning getting hit in the various weak points (chest, solar plexus, liver, etc) and breathing through it. This helps develop the mind to relax when these shots happen and to develop the mental fortitude to keep going when something is uncomfortable.
- Start with doing 50 of these during your regular sit-ups. You want to add 25 every session until you're doing all 300 of your sit-ups while getting hit with the Thai pad.

Chapter Eleven
Sparring Routines

There are so many different types of sparring which I'll describe the ones we use here and when you should be doing them. Sparring in Muay Thai is much safer than sports such as boxing, as the whole body is a target. Thus, emphasis on targeting the whole body while sparring is a MUST, not only the head.

Then the first time of sparring I will describe is what we call "play sparring", the Thai's call it "Len". Play sparring will sometimes take place with & without gloves. There is typically no shin guards used as well. This is to develop accuracy, timing, speed, control & balance. These are all attributes that will play in your favor when taking part in your first Muay Thai fight.

All sparring should be done with an emphasis on SPEED OVER USING POWER. If you can make speed and control the power, you are closer to mastering being able to spar at a higher intensity to mimic a fight with a much lower risk of injury to yourself, but more importantly to your training partners! When using punches, be sure to not be making a fist when sparring to reduce the chance of accidental hard strikes.

Typical Play Sparring Routine, 1-5x per week:
- 4 minute round - kicks only, no catching or blocking kicks, only practicing evasion
- 4 minute round - kicks only, catching OK along with evasion being the priority
- 4 minute round - punch & kick play sparring
- 4 minute round - punch sparring only

The goal of the play sparring routine is it should be something that you could really do every single day. It's fun, it's low pressure and helps develop the fighter's eye vision to spot when to be on offense & when to be on defense. This takes TIME and I highly recommend starting at 20% speed or less if you've never done this time of sparring before to prevent knee collisions & kicking elbows.

The second type of sparring I will describe is what I'll call "technical sparring", which will typically have you in the following equipment:

- Gloves
- Shinguards
- Elbow Pads
- Knee Pads
- Groin Protector
- Mouthpiece
- Optional: Headgear & Chestguard

Preparing For Your First Muay Thai Fight – Vol. 1

For technical sparring, there are many ways to start. When we do technical sparring, this typically takes place in a class setting with students who aren't fighting & competing. Fighters can still get productive work here to develop balance, basics, technique & timing. If you limit yourself to "only fighters", you may find yourself sparring with no one if you are the only fighter in your program. This is ok! You need to learn to develop the rest of those around you as well and this serves as a great opportunity for it. We will designate a speed percentage & a power percentage, for example 20% speed & 10% power. Very rarely do we turn up the power but we will definitely turn up the speed in sparring. This is why "Len" is so important to developing your sparring.

We will use the terminology "3 for 3" or "2 for 2" or "1 for 1" - which simply means that the sparring participants are going 3 strikes for 3 strikes, 2 strikes for 2 strikes, or 1 strike for 1 strike. Often, I'll call for different sequences throughout the sparring in order to develop our students to get used to "hearing" my voice from the corner. It's important that your instructors do this for you so you can learn to hear them as well. When we use the term "Muay Thai Round" we will utilize clinching with very LIGHT straight knees. We typically stick to using the inside "slapping" style of knees that don't cause damage, where you hit with the inside of your thigh not the inside of the knee. We will not be using elbows while sparring, as, in my experience, it's too dangerous, even with elbow pads. You can easily get cut or lose a tooth as elbows start to fly, also elbow pads move a lot!

Typical Technical Sparring Routine, 2-3x per week:

- 2 minute round - 50% speed, 10% power, 3 kicks each, emphasis on blocking & not evasion.
- 2 minute round - 50% speed, 10% power, 3 punches each, emphasis on blocking & evasion.
- 2 minute round - 50% speed, 10% power, 3 strikes punches & kicks only, emphasis on blocking & evasion.
- 2 minute round - 50% to 80% speed, 10% power, kick sparring, emphasis on blocking & evasion, NO CATCHING
- 2 minute round - 50% to 80% speed, 10% power, boxing sparring, emphasis on blocking & evasion.
  - REST
- 3x4 minute rounds - 50% to 80% speed, 10% power, punch & kick sparring, emphasis on blocking & evasion, NO CATCHING
- 3x4 minute rounds - 50% to 80% speed, 10% power, MUAY THAI ROUNDS, emphasis on blocking & evasion, catching allowed.
- 1x4 minute round - 50% to 80% speed, 10% power, boxing only, emphasis on blocking.

The goal of technical sparring is to develop high-intensity sparring utilizing control. Notice how the power never goes up beyond 10%? This is intentional to develop speed over using power. Power is to be developed on the bags & pads and is to be saved for your first Muay Thai fight!

The next type of sparring we will have is Boxing Sparring. Boxing sparring is something we utilize a lot for fighter development as you can typically bring up the power a little bit with a lower chance of injury due to limited limbs flying through space at each other.

Boxing Sparring Equipment:

- Gloves
- Headgear
- Mouthpiece
- Groin Protector

Boxing sparring can be utilized for all students but I'll typically switch fighters between regular students, and paring with each other. A fighter needs to be controlled enough to turn things up and ease up when the instructor calls for such. You want to work to your partner's level. It's safe to assume that power should always stay at 10% but I will show the percentage we push up for our fighters.

Typical Boxing Sparring Routine, 1-2x per week:

- 2 minute round - 50% speed, 10% power, Jab sparring only
- 2 minute round - 50% speed, 10% power, Cross sparring only
- 2 minute round - 50% speed, 10% power, Lead hand punches only
- 2 minute round - 50% speed, 10% power, Rear hand punches only
- 2 minute round - 50% speed, 10% power, 3 for 3
  - REST
- 4 minute round - 50% speed, 50% power, boxing sparring
- 4x4 minute round - 50% to 80% speed, 50% power, boxing sparring

The purpose of the boxing sparring will vary depending on the attribute we want to build. If you're having a hard time staying inside and fighting there, have your partner stay inside with you and focus on small evasion movements and tight defense to counter strike when possible. If you have a tendency to stand and trade, focus on evasive footwork and shutting down your partner's advances. This is a give & take when it comes to sparring and your partner, as well as yourself, must learn to play with each other and try different things. Again, this brings up the importance of "Len" play sparring.

Next on the list is Competition Prep sparring! This is the type of sparring that will help "mock" competition in the sense of being in a ring as well as having your instructors on hand to give coaching advice. We usually designate a student who is training to become a ring official through our program to work as a referee during this time as well. We use the same principle of technical sparring, but now we wear all of the gear that the competition will require. If it's a professional fight or a fight with no shin guards, we will still wear shin guards. Competition Prep sparring should take place once per week and can consist of fighters and other students who are willing to help push the fighters. We implement a Leadership team to help facilitate this as they are people who want to help develop others to a higher standard, which includes fighters.

Typical Competition Prep Sparring Routine:

- Technical Sparring Routine
- 3-5x4 minute rounds - Muay Thai Rounds, a new person every round, adjusting to each person's level, style & intensity while listening to your instructor.
  - If you don't have a ring, some rope strung around 4 points to make a square will do to mimic controlling a square, similar to a ring.

Between every round, you will come to the corner to mimic what competition will be like. It is preferable that those in attendance cheer and make a noise similar to a competition setting. Only the designated instructors should be giving the advice to refrain from an overload of information for the athlete and so that they are able to hone in on the instructor's voice during training. If you can do this while training, you will have a MUCH EASIER TIME when it comes to your first Muay Thai fight! This is a skill and takes practice. So use this time to practice listening to your instructor & corner.

It's important to understand this as well: you will have good and not-so-good sparring sessions. It's a part of the game and part of the mental prep. Some of my best performances were when I got smashed or had a bad sparring session as my last session. The point is to remember the GOOD SESSIONS and reflect on anchoring everything you did which you'll learn a good routine called "Legs Up The Wall" in a different chapter. Try to focus on what worked during sparring sessions when you are winding down and reflect on what you could do better.

Chapter Twelve
Clinching Routines

When it comes to training for your first Muay Thai fight, this is a very important and often neglected part of training. You might be thinking, "well, if it's so important, why is it neglected?" The best way I can relate it to others is that not everyone likes to eat their vegetables when they are a kid but often are forced to by our parent (instructor in this case). For myself, I love clinching and we didn't have the option to clinch when I first started. This wasn't because I didn't want to, just the fact that no one knew how to practice it or teach it. The first time I went to Thailand, I didn't know shit about clinching. When it came time for me to fight on the short stay, rather than teach me to clinch, the Thai trainer I had just told me, "You, no clinch ok? Clinch you lose". Well, lucky for me I didn't know how to clinch. You may be in a similar situation, so I'll describe a little bit for you on how you can practice clinching safely, as well as some routines. I will not go into detail about technique & hand positioning as that can be a whole book in and of itself.

The purpose of clinching is to strike your opponent with knees & elbows, off-balance to set up strikes, to throw or sweep using legal Muay Thai techniques as well as a defensive measure if you're hurt, and as an offensive measure if you're stronger than your opponent there. If you are competing as an amateur and have to wear shinguards, chances are you won't have padding on your knees when you have your first Muay Thai fight. So it makes sense to learn even more for your first fight, not to mention how important it is as you continue to fight & compete in Muay Thai. Clinching is also the best way to improve your body strength & balance for Muay Thai.

How to "Knee" safely & stand while Clinching:

- When you practice clinching, I recommend never use straight knees, especially for beginners as it's too easy to injure your partner.

- When we practice knees, we practice striking with the inside of the thigh. You can practice the same motion as a round knee, but instead of hitting with the inside of the knee joint, we use the mid-thigh to "slap" our partner's body. This translates well to utilizing round knees which will help develop offense inside of the clinch range as well as building your balance.

- When clinching, you should adjust your stance to what we call a "clinch stance" in our programs. Both feet should be shoulder-width and directly under your shoulders, while you maintain being high on your toes. This is to maintain balance and stay in a position to knee at all times.

- When you knee your partner using this style of practice, you should not be hitting the head. This is strictly for use on the body & legs of your partner.

Typical Clinching Routine:

- 1x5 minute rounds - continuous clinch sparring with emphasis on "flowing" and not resisting too much on positions. Emphasis on balance, hand positioning, and staying active with your knees. No elbows, throws, dumps, or sweeps.
- 2x5 minute rounds - no break, live clinch sparring with throws, dumps & sweeps, NO ELBOWS. Get a new partner every round. Repeat for more than 2 rounds if necessary.

This is the basic clinching routine that we will do to get continuous practice. This is about 15 minutes of clinch training every time we do this. If you want to train more clinching, just do additional rounds. As we get closer to ramping up training, we will follow our typical clinching routine with what we call the "Man In The Middle" clinching routine. Man in the middle clinching is used to develop a strong emphasis on building conditioning, stamina as well as mental toughness. This drill is where we "go hard", it should be intense and mimic fighting. We will use this routine while ramping up for a fight. The last time we use this drill will be 1 week away from a fight as part of peak training with trusted training partners.

Man In The Middle Clinching Routine:

- There should be groups of 3 people, 1 person is the "man in the middle" for a 6 to 10 minute round.
- The 2 people will rotate every 1.5-2 minutes. If one of them is thrown, swept or dumped, the other person immediately comes in and starts a new timer.
- If the "Man In The Middle" is thrown to the ground, it is important that the pace is pushed on them as they are most likely behind and must work towards pushing themselves at this point.
- The person on the outside should be watching directly next to the group and keeping an eye on the time. It is that person's responsibility to keep track of time.
- Repeat for the whole group. Yes, you will be tired.

I'd like to close this chapter by saying that clinching is arguably the most important part of training for your first Muay Thai fight. Since it's so neglected, it's easily one of the strongest things a new fighter can bring to the table. It can be very tiring for your opponent if they aren't as strong as you in the clinch. You can tell how strong your opponent is in the clinch as soon as you end up in the clinch range and you grab on. It's also not fun being on the other side of not being strong enough in the clinch. The focus should always be on actually throwing knees. I see way too many people get fascinated with throws, dumps & sweeps because they look cool. Yes, they can be demoralizing but they don't cause nearly as much damage as a strong knee to the gut will inflict.

Chapter Thirteen
Post-Training Stretches For Focus & Flexibility

At the end of every session, there should be a good stretching routine. Some of this stretching routine will bleed over to a part of your warm-ups for fight day to help build focus. Flexibility is important to help keep the body relaxed to conserve energy during strikes. If you're straining for a strike rather than being relaxed, naturally you will expend more energy than if you are relaxed.

Basic Post-Training Stretch Routine:

- Left/Right arm across the chest, pull to stretch, hold for 10 count each side
- Left/Right arm behind head, pull down, hold for 10 count each side
- Feet together, reach up, then down to the floor, hold for 10 count
- Both feet out to the side, reach overhead, hold for 10 count each side
- Hands together, reach down to the floor between legs, hold for 10 count
- Reach to left side/right side, hold for 10 count both sides
- Reach to the floor again and stretch between your legs, hold for 10 count
- Take a seat, butterfly stretch with feet together, try to press knees to ground, and hold for 10 seconds. Have someone

put slight pressure on your legs to increase the intensity of the stretch.

- Both feet out to the side, reaching to the middle/left/right, hold 10 seconds each direction.
- One leg in, reaching over to the extended leg, trying to get your forehead to your knee, hold for 10 seconds each side.
- Extend both legs together, feet out in front, reach down to touch toes, hold for 10 seconds

NOTE: gradually increase stretching times for 5 seconds every session and practice breathing during the stretches while increasing intensity.

Along with this stretching routine, it is a requirement that each of my fighters meditate during stretching. We institute the Viparita Karani pose from yoga, that's a fancy word for putting your legs up the wall to stretch your legs, hips, low back and to open up your chest. Just being straight with you, we just call it "legs up the wall stretch". When I say "meditate" I don't mean sitting cross-legged and humming "om" either. When you meditate, your main objective is to be present and in the moment. We utilize focusing on the sensation of the breath to help facilitate this.

Basic Legs Up The Wall Routine:

- Start by laying on the ground, with your bottom against the wall. With your body perpendicular to your legs running along the wall.
- Take a deep inhale, exhale and open up your arms to lay on your back while kicking your legs up the wall.
- You want your heels on the wall, making sure your lower back is on the ground.
- Scoot back from the wall if necessary to keep your lower back on the floor
- While in this position, the main thing is to focus on the breath.
- While you inhale through your nose, focus on feeling the air intake through your nostrils, through your sinuses, to the back of your throat and into your lungs.
- Focus on expanding the breath into the stomach first, then as your stomach fills up, expand the breath into your chest.
- Exhale slowly, exhibiting the feelings of the breath in reverse through to your mouth.
- With each breath, you want to focus on nothing else but being upside down with your legs on the wall and being present. Whatever it is around you, acknowledge it and let it be. This is an important focus anchor we use prior to competition.
- Focus anchors help you get mentally prepared before a competition to mimic training moments where you were

100% focused and present in the moment. We will talk about this more later.

You want to start off with 5 minutes at the end of every session. Build up to 15 minutes at the end of every session to unwind from training. You have to do this every single day for the final 3 weeks leading up to your first Muay Thai fight!

The purpose of the Legs Up The Wall routine is to help build focus, relax the body & mind. The idea behind this stretch is to get blood & your lymphatic system flowing. Your lymphatic system is part of your recovery system from a hard training session, not to mention your legs will be sore from all of the work you've been putting in towards having your first Muay Thai fight.

Chapter Fourteen
Rest & Recovery

Rest & Recovery are important parts of preparing for your first Muay Thai fight. They are part of the building blocks for having success at anything, even outside of Muay Thai. When in Thailand, you'll see that the fighters sleep, A LOT. Morning training is usually followed up with a nap after eating and prior to afternoon training. There are significant studies showing how intertwined sleep & your hormones are related.

If you think about training as a "stressor" on your body, as you are putting a strain on your body through all that is entailed with training. In order for your body to recover, it will require ample rest & recovery. Sleep is one of the key components of this! We will utilize the Legs Up The Wall routine to help us facilitate unwinding at the end of the day as well as a way to focus. This is especially helpful if you're having a hard time "turning off" your mind before going to bed, especially fight week jitters.

As a general rule of thumb, you will want to aim for between 8-10 hours of sleep per night when training. Every person is different but I found that when I slept less than 8 hours, I would massively under-perform and "gas out" during training when I should be getting ready to peak. I found that 9 hours of sleep is the ideal time frame of sleep in order for me to perform. A training journal is what helped me diagnose what works best for me. I noticed that the days that I was doing everything I should to prepare, I would under-perform when I slept less than 9 hours. When I slept at least 9 hours, I would have massive energy and some of the best sessions and performance in training. So you will have to do some experimenting to see what works for you.

You'll often hear the term "over-training" thrown around, but I feel that this is a way of justifying an athlete for "under-recovering". So if you're feeling burnt out on training and not sure why, take a look at your sleep!

I also highly suggest the use of Epsom salt soaks to help relax your body during your training cycles. You'll find that your body gets overly tight throughout the week, even WITH stretching. This is normal, the Thai method would suggest a massage, and if you can afford to get a legitimate Thai massage (not a rub & tug) then definitely include that into your regime. If you're in Thailand, they are very affordable and you want to consider this as part of your training costs. Back to Epsom salts.

With Epsom salt soaks, it's best if you can do a complete submersion in a bathtub. If you don't have a bathtub, even just soaking your feet in a mixture of Epsom salt and warm water will have benefits. You can also soak a towel in this solution and place it on the areas that you are most tight. The main thing we are looking at getting our body to do is to relax. Epsom salt is high in Magnesium which is the mineral that is responsible for the opposite of muscle contraction: relaxation! After your Epsom salt treatment, I highly suggest some deep & relaxing stretching as your muscles will be much more supple after the soak. A good time for Legs Up The Wall as well. We aim to do this 1-2x per week depending on how fatigued your body feels.

Hydration is also a key factor to recovery and I'll touch more on that in another chapter. As a general rule of thumb, you'll want to aim for drinking AT LEAST 1 gallon of purified water every day. With the amount of training and work you'll be doing, you want to make sure to keep your body well hydrated to prevent unnecessary fatigue & cramping. I prefer some Coconut water (unsweetened) in a can or directly from the coconut if possible. This is to not be confused with coconut milk, they are very different. Coconut water contains a very good mixture of electrolytes (minerals) that will help you rehydrate at a faster rate than just plain water. Think of it as a rehydration supplement.

On top of all of this, it's important that you can unwind from your day, no matter what may be stressing you. When I use the word stress, remember that training is a form of stress on your body. Your sleep will help you recover and train harder the next day. I've found that having a hobby outside of Muay Thai can help you stay relaxed on your "off day" on Sunday or during your downtime. I personally will hang with some friends or my wife at the beach, go for a low-intensity hike, read a book, make some food, spend time with your family, etc.

Chapter Fifteen
Diet & Healthy Habits

I hesitated to use the word "diet" in here as very rarely are fighters on a "diet". Fighters will go onto a regimented diet as fight time approaches to trim down extra water weight as Muay Thai is a weight class based sport. Your relationship to gravity & the Earth matter in preparing for your first Muay Thai fight, so you have to plan accordingly.

The term I prefer to use is "healthy habits", as this is a better reflection of what we instill in our fighters. Healthy habits are things that we maintain year-round and make choices based on long-term health & growth as martial artists. Diets, however, are not year-round and are short-term. Healthy habits include your dietary intake! There are definitely a few books out there that cover this topic in extreme detail and I highly suggest you pick these up.

Living Lean by Mike Dolce
- A healthy lifestyle book full of shopping lists, recipes and ways to instill healthy habits

The Dolce Diet: 3 Weeks To Shredded by Brandy Roon & Mike Dolce
- A weight cutting guide for competitive athletes that is instilled on the protocols outlined in Living Lean.

Preparing For Your First Muay Thai Fight – Vol. 1

These two books are something I find constantly recommending to our fighters when they first approach me about dietary intake and building a healthy lifestyle. I found these books after I'd been experimenting for some time and feel they most accurately reflect what I've found to work for both myself & my fighters.

Personally, I've been experimenting with a completely plant-based diet for the past year as of writing this book. I had a poor experience with it before where I faced issues of low energy but my weight was good or the opposite, which was my weight was high (bad for Muay Thai) and high energy! I feel like it's definitely taken me some time and I've adjusted to a completely plant-based diet at this time. My energy has gone up exponentially and my weight remains closer to where I like to be in regards to Muay Thai. I recommend exploring this option, not to mention the two books mentioned above have vegetarian & vegan options written into the books.

Other things to consider in regards to healthy habits are making sure you take time to "recharge" your energy level. Focusing 100% on Muay Thai 24/7/365 is great and all, but you're bound to need to recharge. It's important that you balance having some social, mental, spiritual & physical outlets to allow yourself to cross-train yourself. The benefits of cross-training will make you recharged and excited about Muay Thai again! This is especially important for after your first Muay Thai fight, to be able to maintain normalcy and keep your emotions at bay.

Chapter Sixteen
Making Weight

I'm not a doctor and I don't recommend you do any extreme weight-cutting or dehydration to make weight. With that said, it's a very real part of preparing for your first Muay Thai fight, making weight. If you follow this book for your training as close as possible, along with the books above I recommended, you should have no issue losing weight. There are exceptions to that rule and in my experience, women have a much harder time losing temporary weight than Men do. I've had a healthy stable of Women fighters, and some have no issues but quite a few were doing more than enough to make weight but still struggled all of the way to the scale.

I really like the breakdown in "The Dolce Diet: 3 Weeks To Shredded" book on how to taper the week of the fight. I highly suggest you read that book for any weight-loss challenges you may be facing.

Tips for trimming down for weigh-in:

- **Sleep A LOT**
  - If you add 1-3 extra hours onto your schedule as your body will most likely need it from the hard training anyways. Weigh yourself before bed, and in the morning when you are naked and before you eat or drink anything. I instruct my athletes to do this every

Wednesday morning to ensure they are mid-way through the training week and have had a few hard sessions by that point as well as some roadwork to make sure they aren't holding onto excess water.

- **Train at a higher intensity for shorter periods leading up to the fight.**
  - I outlined this in a previous chapter in what your last week of training will look like. We do this to allow you to consume fewer calories, empty your bowels & burn excess fat.

- **Jacuzzi over Sauna**
  - If an athlete needs to sweat, I highly recommend a jacuzzi over a Sauna. This has to do with basic chemistry and biology. Your body will sweat to cool itself off. If you're in a dry sauna, then your body will have a tendency to sweat and stop at some point, because of multiple factors, but mostly because your body has done its job of sweating already! The humidity in a dry sauna is close to 0%. If you prolong this, your body catches on and will make it even harder to sweat. With a jacuzzi, the humidity surrounding your body is 100%, you're submerged in water! Not to mention hot water that wicks away the sweat at an accelerated rate due to the humidity level. This allows your body to expel sweat at a significantly faster rate.

- **DON'T USE EITHER TO LOSE WEIGHT**
  - These guidelines are just what I've had to resort to for myself throughout the years to make weight and learned through a lot of trial & error. Success meant

feeling good during fight time, error meant feeling like complete shit during my fight. Results of the fight usually reflected how I was feeling and believe me, I made A LOT of errors.

- **Drink A LOT of water!**
  - I mentioned drinking at least a gallon of water while training. We typically ramp up water intake during the last week of training to help manipulate our bodies to release excess water. I won't get into the science (there is a science behind it) but it works. A simple search for "water loading" will give you a ton of ideas. Please be careful.
- **Sit close to your fight weight**
  - By close, I mean within 10 lbs (~4.5 kgs) to help with this process. Healthy habits & proper training are key here to maintain this.

The Thai method of weight cutting is a very old school method and it works. It involves sweatsuits, running & starving. I really don't recommend it unless that's your only option. My friend Matt Lucas has a great book called, "On Fighting In Thailand" that I recommend which covers this process briefly. Really, I recommend the books in the "Diet & Healthy Habits" chapter for this, as a healthier approach is always better over the long-term. I'm sure you would agree with that as well but sometimes you have to do what you have to do. It's part of competing in Muay Thai!

Chapter Seventeen
Mental Prep & Pre-Fight

As you get into fight week, you may be feeling a few nerves throughout the week. Know that it's completely normal. Every fighter in existence goes through this, from 0 fights to 100+ fights, more experienced fighters just get better at managing it over time. There are multiple things to consider for yourself. In this chapter, I will cover some concepts for you to keep in mind to help better wrap your head around preparing for your first Muay Thai fight!

The first thing to remember is that your mind can play tricks on you! Think about how old you are, that's how long you've built up habits in your mental state that will come up. Feelings of self-doubt are completely normal and to be expected to happen at some point. If you figure you're 25 years old for example, that's 25 years of your life where you've never had your first Muay Thai fight. Of course, your mind is going to be telling you, "What the hell are you about to do?" Something that is important to remember during these moments, is that you've prepared since DAY 1 to do this. In reality, you've trained for a good chunk of time solely for fight day. You figure 3-8 weeks is probably the range you prepared for; sometimes more, sometimes less. Remind yourself of this when you are getting fight week jitters. Remind yourself, "I have prepared fully for this and it's ok if I'm nervous. I've gone my whole life without experiencing this." It really helps to say that out loud.

The second thing to remember is that you might not get nervous at all. But know that it can hit people all at once or in waves. Whether it be on the scale, driving to the fight event, when you see your opponent, seeing the ambulance at ringside, getting checked by the doctor, walking into the ring or when the bell rings for the round to begin. When these moments hit, it's important to remind yourself, "this is what I want to do! I trained so hard for this, enjoy it." That affirmation is something you should be repeating in your head during your Legs Up The Wall routine. This will help to instill a focus anchor into ourselves, as you will be deeply relaxed doing the Legs Up The Wall routine. It's important to draw that calmness you have at the end of your training or end of your day into that present moment. This is something I constantly remind my fighters of as they go throughout their day and is something my coaches I've trained up to work very well with our fighters as well. This helps to instill focus & confidence into the fighter.

The third thing to remember is that you will never "feel prepared" enough for your first fight. The first fight is part of the learning process to learn how to better prepare yourself in the future. Trust in your instructor's confidence in you to be able to fight if they are putting you in to fight. Trust in the hard work you've put in to prepare! It's a constant thing I see with first time fighters. There is usually some acting out like a baby, spazzing out after sparring because they are frustrated, crying, etc... After they calm the fuck down, I usually hear these words, "I don't think I'm ready." Usually, my response is, "I've been doing this a long time, so trust me, you're ready." It's important that you know this about your instructor, if they are worth their weight, they will be straight up with you. I've seldom had fighters that I didn't feel were prepared after going through the competition preparations we have here in this book. I have a great memory of one of our champion's first fights, it was after the last sparring session and I went to teach my next class. I heard crying by our boxing ring and went back to see who it was and what happened. It was our first-timer, Joanna, about to fight next weekend. Her words, "I don't feel like I have any power" and she was literally 105 lbs soaking wet, she has the power of a 125-pound woman. I reassured her she is more than ready to fight in a tournament the following weekend. Guess what happened? ...First-round TKO via punches! She went onto the finals to fight a much more skilled and heavier opponent where she went the distance of the whole fight! Talk about a confidence booster. She went on to win a National Title as well as being ranked #1 in her weight-class here in North America as an amateur competing with IFMA competitors and high ranked fighters.

The fourth thing to remember is to ENJOY THE FUCKING EXPERIENCE! I see so many people who get anxious and rush themselves into the warm-up and the ring. It's important to remember how much time this goes into fight preparations. Fight night is the time for you to enjoy the moment and "take it all in." It will be over so fast, so it's important to not rush things. When you get nervous, remind yourself how much this is something you want to be doing and how hard you prepared for this. Be present and in the moment. Get your mind anchored back into when you were training and about to get ready for a badass sparring session where everything just "clicked".

The fifth thing to remember is that you should know how to win and know how to lose. What does this mean? It means that you may feel like you won sometimes but the judges saw it another way. It's not the end of the world, be a good sportsman, that's part of what makes Muay Thai special. When you win, smile, and be a good sportsman to your opponent no matter their attitude. No matter the circumstances, enjoy it and be a good sport, as that will help you to gain more fans down the road which will be very important.

The sixth thing to remember is that it is all about you for however long that fight is. Do your best to stay focused and present in the ring. If you're not a selfish person, this can be hard. I highly suggest you practice being selfish during sparring rounds where you ONLY FOCUS ON YOU, this is a big reason for Competition Prep sparring. You must focus on nothing but you. I've seen this throw a wrench in some badass fighters who had something going on in their minds, which leads me to...

The seventh thing to remember is that you can't hide shit from your instructors when you are preparing for a competition. Nervous? Share it with your instructor, they can coach you through it. Have some personal problems? Share it with your instructor so you can get it off your chest and they know where your head is at. Constipated after weigh-in or diarrhea? ...Share that information with your instructor, they can advise from there and understand what's going on. I know it's a lot of personal stuff, but no one cares and it's probably nothing new to your instructor. If you hide this kind of stuff or don't share it with your instructor, chances are you will mentally fuck yourself up and your instructor can't help because they won't know what is going on.

The eighth thing to remember is that no matter what happens, your instructor is equally as invested as you are. They took just as much time to help you prepare and show up to the fight event. I say this because fights do "drop out" from an even last minute. I saw this happen with a fighter when my Thai instructor was training us. The fighter started cursing and saying how much of a waste of time this was for HIM and how mad HE WAS and how HE WOULD NEVER TRY TO FIGHT AGAIN. Please realize that this is the wrong kind of selfishness. You don't want that. Your instructor is equally as upset, even if they don't show it. It's a big sacrifice of their time & body as well, something they will never get back.

The ninth thing to remember is that you need to pack some food and snacks! Don't eat anything you wouldn't normally eat. If you don't normally eat ice cream before sparring, don't cram ice cream down your throat after weigh-in... Save that crap for after your fight. I've seen fighters self-sabotage themselves. I've seen inexperienced coaches encourage fighters to eat Fettuccine Alfredo on a same-day weigh-in with only a few hours between fights... "what the fuck" was what I said when I heard this. It's important to save new experiments for training and after your fight, not when you prepared so hard for so long for this moment.

The tenth thing to remember is that you will most likely get really tired. This is from your adrenaline dumps that happen throughout the event, leading up to your first Muay Thai fight as well as during. That's why it's so important to anchor those calm moments using the Legs Up The Wall routine.

While you are warming up, it should be light as if you were preparing to do some hard sparring! Maybe some pads with your instructor, stretching & shadowboxing. You want to make sure you have all of your required equipment. I usually just instruct our fighters to bring all of their sparring gear, just in case something is missing.

If you find yourself getting anxious and you have a lot of time still, then do the Legs Up The Wall routine in the warm-up area. It's ok, everyone else has their own way of doing things, this is how we do it. It's important to realize that many of the people around you might be trying to figure this shit out and didn't buy this book. You'll see some crazy stupid shit like hitting themselves, jumping up and down, chugging energy drinks, etc. It's very important to stay as relaxed as possible until it's time for you to actually fight! Trust your instructors will help you prepare and be ready when you need to be but also be self-aware of these things as well.

If possible, I highly suggest getting into the ring you will be competing in before the event and do some light shadowboxing and visualizing your movements & strikes around the ring. This can help to further anchor yourself to that point in time. That way when you get into the ring later, it's nothing new, you've been there already! You know what is going to happen. It will just be time to execute.

Chapter Eighteen
Your First Muay Thai Fight

If you do everything in this book, you will feel successful no matter the outcome. You were dedicated, disciplined and you put in the time. Those three very important things we covered at the beginning of this book, not to mention your "why". Your "why" is what you need to remind yourself when stepping into the ring. You anchored your "why" mentally using the Legs Up The Wall routine and are able to recenter and make yourself present. You have been "in the zone" in that "flow state" during sparring and tonight is your night to be there as well.

Do your best to listen to your corner, stay focused, stay relaxed, and try not to think too much. Be present and trust in your training! If you trust in your training, you will just "go" and do what you are supposed to. Of course, that is as long as you can stay focused and present. Control those adrenaline dumps and enjoy the post-fight celebration! Remember that things will happen that are out of your control, let that shit go and keep doing what you do best. You're doing something that such a small percentage of people in the world will do, but you're ready to go! You've got this!

Closing Thoughts

This book has been a long time coming and I hope you enjoy the experience you are able to take with you into your first Muay Thai fight. It's a big feat to step into the ring! I've seen badass people who never step foot into the ring because they lack dedication, discipline & time! So when you get there, be sure to celebrate all of the hard work you've done to make this happen. Get back physically into your program as soon as possible. Whether it be to just hang out with your team or getting back to training. It's your turn to give back to the program that helped you get to the ring and if you aren't there, there is not much of a team after everyone fights. I see it all of the time... See you at the tournaments.

Be sure to tag us on Facebook & Instagram @PuuMuayThai and use the hashtag #PreparingForYourFirstMuayThaiFight for your post-fight picture! We will share it and give you a free shout-out on social media.

Stay happy & stay healthy!

Jonathan Puu
Founder, Pu'u Muay Thai Inc.

Made in the USA
Monee, IL
29 August 2022

12801807R00046